Stone Arch Bridge   South Hadley, Massachusetts   Henry G. Peabody

The Connecticut River

In the summer of 1900, Henry G. Peabody stood on a point on Mt. Holyoke (opposite page) and photographed the panorama of the Connecticut River which appears on the fold-out pages.

This particular stretch of the river (which flows from right to left in the photo) is regarded as one of the more scenic river valleys in New England and has been the subject of many American landscape paintings. It has also been one of the most utilized for farming and related industries.

Since 1900, the river has cut its curve, at right in photo, much farther to the right, destroying the roads on the east bank. The point-bar inside the curve is known as "Rainbow Beach," colored by the bands of decayed forest growth.

The pilings crossing the river below the curve were anchors for a boom that gathered logs which lumbermen had cut in New Hampshire and Vermont. The logs were stored behind Shepard's Island, on the opposite side of the river.

The broad flood-plain meadow at Northampton, "The Meadow City," appears as the sparsely treed area in the center of the photo. Settlers invaded the flood plain in the 1630s to farm the soil made fertile through the deposition of minerals by annual floods. For centuries before the arrival of Europeans, the Nonotuck Indians farmed the rich flood plain. The valley was the scene of many conflicts between whites and Indians because both recognized it as highly productive land.

On the near shore, at lower left, is the village of Hockanum and the Hockanum Ferry. The ferry, which is tied at dock in the photo, was hand-drawn by cable across the river. It operated long after a bridge was built between Hadley and Northampton.

On the left is the famous "Ox Bow," a channel which the Connecticut River abandoned in 1841, when a flood rose over a narrow neck of land and cut a shorter channel. The old channel became a lake which, at the time of this picture, was used for storage of logs and was the site of a major paper mill. Booms in the lower part of the picture gathered logs which were moved into the Ox Bow. The paper mill is on the left side of the island in the middle of the Ox Bow, and stored logs can be seen floating in front of the mill.

Leaving this stretch, the river passes through a water gap at the lower left in photo between Mt. Tom and Mt. Holyoke. The gap is the subject of one of the more splendid and moody landscapes of the Hudson River School, painted by Thomas Cole in 1836. The painting, now in the Metropolitan Museum of Art in New York City, was done five years before the river cut off the Ox Bow, and the narrow neck of the bend is striking.

Logs no longer run on the river. Instead, three marinas and a state boat launch make this stretch of river an important recreation area. Massachusetts Audubon's Arcadia Wildlife Sanctuary, with its recent Ned's Ditch acquisition, can be seen on the opposite end of the Ox Bow.

Robie Hubley, Director
Arcadia Wildlife Sanctuary

We did not see it coming across the woodlot, pasture, cornfield,
　　to a sagging doorstep and a rickety child; nor in the miles-
　　long furrows only machines could plow, the wheatfields
　　horizon-wide which only machines could harvest.
We did not see it, when, abandoning our hard-won farms to
　　sink among impoverished fields, we moved to cities, wiped
　　soot from windows fronting on blank walls, saw children
　　with only vacant lots to play in, fled in summer the rooms
　　and pavements no night wind came to cool, took trains and
　　trolleys to line's end, carrying our babies and our lunches,
　　to find only some meager green, some dirty beach.
We did not see it when, moving out—for a breath of air,
　　a smell of grass, a sight of the new moon through leaves—
　　into wave after wave of suburbs, we found ourselves still
　　facing windows, bounded by backyards, watching the trees,
　　brooks, meadows we came for vanish beneath more suburbs.
Even on holidays we did not see it when, thinking that in
　　automobiles we had found at last a way back to the skies
　　and spaces, we jammed the highways, moved bumper to
　　bumper, inch by inch, past suburbs, industries, junkyards,
　　evil marshes, burning refuse, until, weary, desperate, the
　　day half gone, we turned off at the first shine of leaves
　　or glint of water—and crashed through saplings, tore flowers
　　and branches, threw trash, polluted streams, scared birds
　　and beasts away from helpless young, and left unquenched
　　sparks that the next breeze fanned to flame.

"This Is the American Earth," Ansel Adams and Nancy Newhall

Farmlands Two: The Technologic Flaw

It is often salutary to re-examine one's immediate concerns in a broader perspective. Most of the land use problems with which environmentalists are concerned —drainage, suburbanization, highways, airports, mining, over-grazing, clear-cutting, and the like —are basically problems of unwise use or overuse of land. But underlying these is a more general problem, another symptom of which is unwise disuse of land. For almost every family that leaves the cities to settle in the suburbs or in a coastal or desert resort, another poorer family leaves the countryside to seek a living in the cities.

Statistics speak for themselves. In 1940 nearly 31 million persons lived on farms in the United States. Assuming a rate of increase similar to that of the population as a whole, this segment of population should have increased to more than 49 million by 1974. In fact, however, the farm population is now scarcely larger than

By I.C.T. Nisbet
Member of the Massachusetts and National Audubon Joint Scientific Staff. Nisbet is a physicist with special knowledge of biology.

9 million. It is no coincidence that the number of people living in cities with populations greater than 25,000 grew from 45 million to 96 million in the same period. This great population shift from the farms to the cities represents a social upheaval almost without parallel since the great migrations from European farms to North American farms in the last century. Its primary cause is the industrialization of agriculture— a technological revolution which, although widely overlooked even by informed social commentators, probably has had more profound social consequences than any of the other technological innovations of the 20th Century.

Environmentalists traditionally have avoided taking strong positions on agricultural policy. Despite the obvious importance of farmland as wildlife habitat, and its potential for multiple-use recreation, conservationists have generally treated a farmer's use of his own land as his own business. Conflicts have arisen primarily where agricultural practices have affected public resources away from the farm— e.g., through enclosure of public land for grazing, diversion of water supplies, drainage of waterfowl habitat, poisoning of predators, shooting of migratory

birds, or use of persistent mobile pesticides. Even some important off-site effects, such as siltation, salinization, or pollution from agricultural wastes, have received less attention than they deserve. This "hands-off" policy is now badly in need of review.

Pesticides provide a revealing example. Environmentalists have rarely opposed the use of non-persistent pesticides in agriculture; indeed, most environmentalists specifically endorse the use

of short-lived pesticides in judicious quantity as part of integrated control programs. The pesticide controversies of the past have been concerned largely with non-agricultural uses (against forest insects, mosquitoes, etc.) and/or with the persistent pesticides and their pervasive off-site effects. The environmentalists' long campaigns against these persistent chemicals are now beginning to achieve success, with the recent cancellation of registrations of

DDT, impending cancellations of aldrin and dieldrin, and reductions in use of others. Yet it is unlikely that these successes could have been so complete if there had been serious evidence that the pesticides provided solid and genuine economic benefits in agriculture.

It became clear during the cancellation hearings that these chemicals—whatever their original short-term success—no longer controlled their target pests and were in many cases doing more harm than good. Despite the massive evidence of environmental damage, it became obvious that the greatest sufferers were the farmers and farmworkers themselves—trapped on the "chemical treadmill" in which every application made the crop more susceptible to attack, and the farmer more dependent on the chemicals and their salesmen. The consequence of 30 years of chemical "control" is that many crops—e.g., cotton, corn, apples, and tobacco—can only be grown economically with repeated applications of pesticides, a system in which it is too complicated and expensive for the small farmer to compete.

Pesticides comprise only a small component of the agro-industrial revolution. The great goal of "efficiency" in agriculture—narrowly defined as obtaining the maximum crop yield from each acre in relation to the economic input—has been achieved primarily through the development of new crop varieties. In most cases the varieties selected were those that respond best to heavy applications of fertilizer, and improved yields are closely correlated to investments in fertilization. Economic analysis suggests that pesticides make only a limited contribution to crop yields, but they permit planting of extensive monocultures which are "efficient" to plant, fertilize, and harvest. The replacement of human labor by mechanical and chemical treatment means that it is now possible to grow many crops with only 10 to 20 human visits to the fields per year. At the same time traditional animal husbandry has been progressively replaced by "factory farming," in feedlots and batteries. Together these trends have led to a desolate emptiness in the agricultural landscape which is uncanny to those who can recall the human and animal activity on farms 30 or 40 years ago. The trends are far from complete, but agriculture already has been largely transformed from an "inefficient" labor-intensive occupation to an "efficient" capital-intensive industry.

The industrialization in producing food has of course been matched by industrialization of processing, packaging, and marketing. The nutritional quality and flavor of present-day packaged foods, and the hazards posed by food additives, are matters of much dispute, but the short-term economic efficiency of the system is clear. (It should be noted, however, that this "efficiency" is achieved at high cost: industrialized agriculture is energy-intensive and American food is among the most expensive in the world; the claims that it is relatively cheap are only justified in relation to per capita income.)

Achievement of efficiency has resulted in serious economic strains. Demand for food is relatively inelastic, and until recently the U.S. was blessed with plenty of good land for its modest population. Hence overproduction of food soon became much more of a hazard to the farmer than underproduction. Agricultural economic policy for long was designed primarily to limit production in order to protect the farmer against falling prices. Production quotas, surplus purchases, export subsidies, food stamp programs, soil banks, and price supports were all tools that were used to this end.

All of these trends—technological and economic—had the same general consequence: to sharpen the competition between the large and small farmer. Introduction of new machinery and new varieties required capital; use of pesticides and fertilizers required both capital and precise knowledge; only those with plenty of land could take it out of production and claim support payments. Agricultural extension agents, charged with improving efficiency, channelled their advice and expertise to the wealthy, middle-class (and white) farmers who seemed most capable of making use of it. Even price supports, introduced ostensibly to offer a fair living to all, paradoxically provided the greatest benefits to those with the lowest

overheads and the greatest ability to switch production into the most profitable crop. Thus the pursuit of efficiency led progressively to the elimination of the landless farmworkers and the small farmers, and their replacement by large industrial-type farms. The final stage in the process is now starting to take place, as the large farms are being taken over by food-processing corporations, by conglomerates, or by corporations diversifying out of other industries. Modern agriculture has no place for the farmer, except as a hired manager of investment.

Apologists for agribusiness claim with pride that the work force in U.S. agriculture has been reduced by a factor of four or five and now comprises only four percent of U.S. labor. Fortunately, the claim is false, because it takes account only of those actually working on farms. If all those engaged in producing food are counted—including, for example, those manufacturing machinery, servicing tractors, producing fuel, transporting produce, producing packaging, processing food, working in supermarkets, etc.— the agricultural work force has been reduced by scarcely half. Even this reduction, however, has been a societal catastrophe. Most of the new jobs created have been for skilled industrial workers; the unskilled workers and their families forced off the land have

been left to fend for themselves and have drifted to the cities. The quest for "efficiency" in agriculture that we have witnessed in the last 30 years has in fact been a systematic, deliberate program to promote an industrialized, capital-intensive system; its success has benefited the rich and skilled, at the expense of the poor.

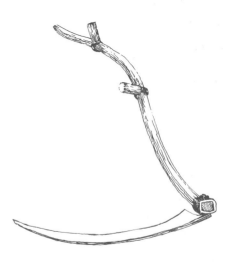

One should not waste too many tears on the way of life that has been destroyed. Despite the nostalgia that it sometimes receives, life on small, poor farms in the early 20th Century was nasty, brutish, and all too often short. The goal of improving the farmer's lot was a worthy one. But the transmutation of rural poverty into urban poverty has not achieved it. Nor has it even eliminated rural poverty: much of the remaining manual work on farms is now performed by migrant laborers whose conditions of life are a well-concealed scandal. There must surely be a third way that could have been—and could still be—better than either. Modern agriculture does not need to be capital-intensive and energy-intensive in order to maintain high productivity and efficiency. A small, diversified farm using the best modern technologies of crop rotation, plant selection, animal husbandry,

integrated pest control, and semi-organic fertilization, can be just as efficient in the true economic sense as the present-day industrialized chemical-food factory. All that is required to promote the modern family farm is the removal or reversal of the huge economic subsidies—direct and indirect—that have favored the large industrial farm for so long. Such a redirection of agricultural policy would have immediate social benefits, and would be a wise and humane policy to meet future social pressures. It is difficult to see how present-day agrotechnology can remain viable in face of likely future crises of energy supply and underemployment.

In expressing these ideas, I have often been asked whether the adverse social effects of agrotechnology should have been foreseen, or were in fact foreseen and inherited. At the very highest

level, the answer is surely yes. It is difficult to avoid apportioning full responsibility to the leaders of the agro-industrial complex who determined the policies—Congressional committees, industry lobbyists, secretaries of agriculture, executives of agribusiness corporations, and top officials in USDA. It would indeed be an insult to the intelligence of these presumably intelligent men to suppose that they could not evaluate and did not weigh carefully the consequences of their decisions. But the actual implementation of the agro-industrial revolution was carried out piecemeal, by researchers at agricultural-experiment stations, by teachers at land-grant colleges, by county extension agents, by salesmen for feed manufacturers, and the like. Most of these people were set relatively narrow goals and often achieved them with distinction; it perhaps would be unreasonable to blame them for not questioning the goals themselves. The aims of increasing "efficiency" and eliminating

"degrading" human labor from the farm were indeed laudable, if divorced from the larger social context.

Even if it should be assumed, charitably, that the adverse social consequences were totally unforeseen, it would not be reasonable to excuse a repetition of the same mistakes. Yet the miracle of development that has been granted to 40 million poor farm residents in the U.S. is now being extended to 400 million peasants in the developing countries. The so-called "Green Revolution" is founded on the same basic technology—high yielding strains of plants requiring heavy applications of fertilizers and pesticides for maximum "efficiency." Little or no thought is being given to evaluating the full social costs of this technology.

Those who have developed these strains and are directing their introduction cannot now claim ignorance and surprise if they displace poor farmers from their lands. Those who advance the capital to finance their introduction cannot now claim to do so out of disinterested benevolence. Here is a real issue for environmentalists.

* Contribution No. 117 from the Scientific Staff, Massachusetts Audubon Society.

The Fertile Valley

As early as 3000 B.C. settlers were filtering into the
Connecticut River Valley, attracted primarily by the rich
soils of its flood plain and the wealth of wildlife in its marshes.
In 1633 A.D. European man moved into the Valley, uprooted
one culture and began to build another. Ironically not much
has changed. Man still farms the flood plain and in some cases
even grows the same crops—corn and tobacco.

The photographs on the following pages were taken by
Hal Morgan, a student of land use at Hampshire College.
Taken as they were after some 5000 years of continuous
habitation they are illustrative of an enduring relationship
that can develop between man and the land. But they are
also something else. There is a certain quality of light and
atmosphere in these photos that seems to linger in river
valleys and around large bodies of open waters.

the place being we think very commodius . . . containing Large quantitys of excelent Land and Meadow and tillable ground sufficient for two larg planttations . . .

Description of the Connecticut River Valley at Northhampton from a petition to the General Court of Massachusetts, 1653.

Urban Land Is Your Land Too

"In the city there is no environment left," commented an environmentalist reflecting a proverbial bias in favor of the countryside and wilderness. But in the city through constant human effort natural processes are pushed into the background. The result at its best can be a human environment more stimulating and rewarding than any other.

But cities are in trouble. An Audubon slide sequence shows progressive environmental deterioration as one travels from the outer suburbs toward the city center. Boston which prides itself as being "the livable city" nevertheless has witnessed such a flight to the suburbs that it has lost 16.6 percent of its population since 1950. After decades of urban renewal, dilapidated housing, boarded-up shops and piles of trash in the streets are not hard to find. Sections of the downtown business district are all but deserted at night. Poverty and overcrowding hardly enhance the quality of life. In many neighborhoods to walk alone after dark is to risk one's safety and one's pocketbook. In creating pleasant

By Scott I. Paradise
Co-director, Boston Industrial
Mission.

Title photo: Reston, Virginia

and stimulating urban environments we hardly have been completely successful.

Cities for Efficient Consumption

An approach to the question may be found in the implications of a book published in 1947 with the inauspicious title *Communitas*. Its authors Paul and Percival Goodman argue that the land use patterns of cities, and therefore to some extent the urban quality of life, depend on the predominant social philosophy of their builders. To illustrate they describe in some detail hypothetical models of varying urban land use patterns. One of these they call the city of efficient consumption. It is dedicated to the proposition that a failure of demand for manufactured goods to keep up with production would pose a major threat to social well-being. Cities built according to this premise must be organized so to be as efficiently wasteful as possible.

The idea that resources might be scarce and that thrift might be required seems utterly foreign to the builders of this city. Instead, the authors suggest, it organizes its land use pattern according to concentric rings. The market, light industry, offices and entertainment coalesce in the urban core. Around this in the next ring gather the institutions of science, higher education and

culture. The third ring attracts the centers of domestic life including elementary schools and neighborhood shops as well as residences. On the outskirts heavy industry crowds along railroad lines and truck terminals. And recreational areas, forestry and truck farms spread over the horizon. This land use pattern was designed to accommodate the highest development of mass production and ease and convenience for mass consumption.

With a shock of recognition we notice, as the authors intended, that this city displays land use patterns not dissimilar to those of the modern American metropolis. Although as a people we place a high value on mass production and consumption, our urban land use patterns may not reflect a conscious ambition to consume wastefully. But if that had been our goal, we would have designed buildings somewhat like steel and glass skyscrapers. We would have been likely to produce a transportation mode, wasteful of land and resources, like the automobile on the urban highway. We would have sought to develop a metropolitan land use pattern similar to ours today. What else could consume more resources than our practice of placing most homes in the suburbs, hundreds of thousands of jobs in the city core and furnishing 200-horsepower cars to transport most jobholders from their beds to their desks each day?

The Goodmans describe the city of efficient consumption as one which can afford life considerable satisfaction. For them the venality of endless consumption could be relieved by a sense of the grandeur of the skyscrapers and pride in the technological accomplishment of keeping the whole complex urban machinery functioning. They even suggested an annual carnival with Dionysian festivities to balance the months of disciplined work in factory and office. One issue, however, escaped their notice. They took it for granted that supplies of material resources would be unlimited. In the year of the energy "crisis," the rising price of food and the dark clouds of a coming age of famines, one wonders if a society is in the long run sustainable if it is based on the assumption of the desirability of waste and the inexhaustibility of resources. We know that physical growth must eventually stop and that even our present high level of consumption may be impossible to maintain. In that case the land use patterns of our cities of efficient consumption are bound to change.

Cities for Economic Exploitation

But to point out the limited future of cities of efficient consumption is not to explain why they suffer such present decrepitude. We must look further. Lewis Mumford once observed that "the city from the beginning of the 19th Century on was treated not as a public institution, but as a private commercial venture to be carved up in any fashion that might increase turnover and further the rise in land values."

To create an orderly land use pattern the city of efficient consumption would have to take shape according to the vision of an urban planning authority. But the contemporary urban area grows through a variety of private economic initiatives influenced only partially by a hodgepodge of government constraints and incentives. Our social philosophy decrees the pre-eminence not only of efficient consumption but also private profit. Our cities are often seen by their citizens more as areas to exploit than as homes to love. City governments often see urban open space and buildings as a source of property tax more than a source of pleasure.

This philosophy of exploitation helps to blur the neat concentric circles patterned for efficient consumption and instead spawns wide areas of decay that appear on no city planner's drawing board. A thousand profitable business decisions begin the process of deterioration. A bank decides that, while accepting deposits from local urban residents, it will refuse applications for home improvement loans from these same residents. Instead the bank lends its money to suburban home owners at less risk. An insurance company cancels an insurance policy for the contents of a home once it has been burglarized. A landlord moves his tenants out and demolishes their homes if he learns the land can yield a higher return in another use.

The property tax often takes blame for urban decay, for through its heavy dependence on this revenue source city governments establish vicious circles which undermine the health of their own community. In order to avoid paying more taxes landlords allow their property to run down. In order to increase their income from the deteriorating property they increase the number of rent payers by overcrowding. In this way without receiving higher tax revenues the city is forced to furnish additional services for the new tenants. This presents the need for higher tax rates to pay for the services. Furthermore, in then desperate need for new tax revenue city governments sometimes endorse industrial and commercial development without considering its effect on the well-being of the community. Thus while bringing in more tax revenues, the city may find even more expenditures for city services are required in the end.

The fiscal plight of the city can be dramatically seen in the decline of its share of tax dollars as compared with the state and federal governments. For instance, in 1932 cities collected more taxes than either the states or the federal government. In 1955 the states collected almost twice as much as the cities and the federal government almost seven times as much. The decline in the cities' share of the tax dollar was exacerbated by the streams of new citizens from the countryside or overseas. All of these required city services and many laid legitimate claims to welfare.

Moreover, increasingly city governments are not altogether able to make their own land use policies. Detroit, for example, larger and less complex than some New England cities, recognizes that five institutions largely determine its future. At least few

major decisions are likely to be sustained over the strenuous objections of the presidents of Ford, General Motors, Chrysler, the United Automobile Workers and the most prestigious head of the downtown businesses. It frequently has happened that none of these men live in the city. Four of them represent national organizations who see the well-being of the city as but a small item on their agendas. Perhaps even worse has been the effect in New England of conglomerates gobbling up local industries to remove the control of each city's economic destiny to some distant boardroom in New York or Dallas.

And public agencies themselves succumb to the demand that the city be exploited for profit. Highway departments have rammed expressways through urban neighborhoods which break up communities and congest feeder streets with suburban commuter cars. A city, less blessed than Boston, demolished its dignified 19th Century city hall because it was expensive to maintain. The site now produces income as a parking lot.

This destruction of urban land and amenities for the sake of the dollar is not inconsistent with our traditional belief that land like other resources is limitless. Why should we maintain property and protect it carefully? There is always more. But it is becoming more apparent that land even more than most other resources is both limited and precious, most limited and precious in the city. When a community condones destructive exploitation of its land it is party to the lie about its finitude; the quality of its environment is bound to suffer.

Cities for Living

A city of efficient consumption and voracious exploitation is not the only urban land use pattern we can imagine for industrial society. The Goodmans describe a second possibility which would tend to reduce the difference between production and consumption. The hypothetical city of efficient consumption, and actual past trends in urban land use, separate the city into areas with specialized functions. As a householder separates cooking, eating and sleeping from each other by assigning each activity its own room, so cities have increasingly developed their own bedroom communities, government centers and financial districts. This land use pattern typically places residences far from most people's work and requires considerable travel not only to and from work but also for recreation and shopping. It often means residential areas seem all but deserted during the day and the downtown business district may be vacated at night.

In *Communitas* the Goodmans describe a city land use pattern which would decentralize the productive process and mix offices and industries in residential neighborhoods. According to this plan the urban milieu would also be enriched with the artful arrangement of housing, offices, shops, restaurants and other amenities

around public squares so as to encourage community interaction. Parts of this vision are echoed and further developed by other writers who argue that the genius of the city is the concentration of various specialized functions in a relatively small area. The modern city tends to create congestion while dispersing specialized function. Wilfred Owen in *The Accessible City* argues that only by a re-ordering of urban land use which places in proximity work, trade and residence can urban transportation problems be solved. This solution does not involve the construction of more transportation facilities so much as reducing the need for travel and this would reduce the consumption of energy at the same time.

In bits and pieces an urban land use pattern similar to that described here already exists. A German city badly bombed in World War II required that every new building constructed include two floors of residences. As a result every block in the city has its inhabitants. No streets are deserted after working hours. And shops and restaurants find patrons in every block. Reston, Columbia and other new towns have been built in part to reflect some of these ideas as have some new city centers such as Atlanta and San Antonio. Boston has the good fortune of retaining some of these characteristics through good luck and good planning. When a mayor can walk to city hall from his home or an insurance company employee can go for a sail during lunch hour a city can claim with some justice that it is livable. But these examples are exceptions to overall trends still pointing toward increasing consumption of goods and continued exploitation of both land and people.

To reverse these trends may not be possible. If possible at all it will require not only better planning but a new philosophy of planning which does not rest on the bankrupt notions of inexhaustible resources, unlimited space and the primacy of economic considerations. Rather, urban planning will have to give priority to an overall improvement of public services and environmental quality. Moreover, unless the residents themselves gain greater control over the destinies of their own cities, cities are likely to remain victims of exploitation by institutions with primary interests elsewhere and commuters with homes in parasitical suburbs.

New policies will also be needed. For instance, alternative income sources must be designed to replace the present heavy dependence on the property tax. A progressive payroll tax may be a partial answer to join with a better means of sharing federal income.

The needs of the cities cannot be met with less. Or again, the automobile, whose accommodation takes up to 35 percent of urban land area, does not belong in city centers. Its entrance must be limited and its parking restricted. An upgrading of public transportation can help satisfy the need for mobility and carefully altered land use patterns can reduce it.

But none of these reforms will likely come about as long as we view the city primarily as a resource to be exploited. We can save it if we know it as a home to be lived in and to love.

The Utopian Illusion

When morning first lights the coast of Maine, the pale forms of sea gulls loom out of the dark. Still invisible crows shout to each other across the cove. Most of the gulls are alone, each on fifty yards of shore. In a few places there are two together. When a passing gull flies over, each gull lowers its head and gives a mewing cry or trumpeting call. Then a chorus of gull calls rises, like conversation at a party, from a flock loafing on the ledge off the end of the point. Hours later, on a last walk along the shore after supper, one can see the gulls back at their shore stations and looking down into the water.

These are the sights and sounds of a peaceful scene where nature appears undisturbed. Many of us yearn for such a condition for ourselves, idealizing it as one in which all members coexist, free of man's competitive rat race. We imagine that we can see in the natural system a resilient struc-

By William H. Drury
Director of the Massachusetts Audubon Scientific Staff, and an acknowledged authority on gulls and several other seabirds.

Illustrated by the author

ture built on mutual accommodation. We *want* to believe that the system fills the needs of all individuals and we can sympathize with the many people, especially the young, who are trying to return to innocent communion with nature—within God's plan.

The desire to find in nature the ideal system that takes care of its own has a venerable tradition. It occurs in the Garden of Eden legend and in the Rousseau ideal of the noble savage. It seems to emerge in the ecological concept of the wilderness climax and again in classical economics as market theory. According to market theory, the feedback of consumer demand regulates the flow of resources and production to all members of society.

But the illusion of natural life on the seashore as a Utopia is progressively dispelled the closer one looks into the lives of gulls. Why are the gulls at the shore in early morning and just before dark? Why are some gulls isolated, and why do they greet each gull that flies over? What does the greeting mean? Why are some gulls cruising? Who are the gulls in the "loafing" flock?

What are the gulls really doing? The gulls are looking for food. Each is trying to feed itself, and also its young ones on the nesting island. The nagging hunger of

the young drives the parents to spend all day hunting, so that just before dark they try to get one more snack for themselves. Even so, the parents raise only a minority of the young that hatch. Two out of three young produced die in the gull colony.

The gulls that have isolated themselves along the shoreline are the dominant ones who can drive out competing gulls. These individuals stand high in the gull hierarchy and respond quickly to any challenge. They greet each passing gull with a warning to "keep going." The mew cry and the trumpeting call express high levels of hostility or aggressiveness. The cruising gulls are hungry ones that are excluded from "the establishment." They are looking for a spot where they can settle and hunt for food without being driven off by the owner. The loafing flock is made up primarily of these drifters (losers) waiting for an easy meal from a passing fishing boat, jostling with each other for status in the meantime.

The seashore, in fact, is a dog-eat-dog society like that of the opening of the West or the 19th Century industrial economy. The picturesque gull floating lightly on the tide pool is the local bully. His life is a continuing struggle to drive out the upstarts that persist in trying to take over. He enjoys affluence as long as he can dominate, but as soon as he lets up, he is "dumped."

The gull population could have a system that was compassionate. Why not ease competition so that all gulls are better off? If each female gull laid only half as many eggs each year and bred only until she had raised two young, gulls might lead less desperate lives.

Why do the gulls not limit their reproduction? The answer lies in the success of those that cheat against the general good. For instance, if most gulls produce two eggs and breed only twice, while a few produce three eggs or breed five times, the pairs that produce more young will contribute more than their share to the inheritance of the next generation. By applying simple arithmetic one can see that the tendency to produce more young would spread through the population. This is the action of natural selection, and it drives gulls to produce as many young as there is any hope of raising.

Thus each animal produces as many young as it can. The population increases until it comes up against the limits set by the resources available. The individual must compete for the limited resources, and certain individuals will be excluded from access because of their low position in the social hierarchy. Thus the major requirement for biological success is for the individual to excel in the social group in which it will survive and reproduce.

Do these observations on other animals have any relevance to humans? In the 115 years since the publication of Darwin's book, *On the Origin of Species,* people have argued about whether humans are "just another animal" or a special creation. In theory, these observations on other animals certainly ought to apply to humans, because natural selection which has controlled the evolution of every other species, also has controlled human evolution. Although language and technology have led to extremely intricate social patterns, one begins by assuming that the individuals who make up the human species are, like the organisms that make up other species, attempting to maximize their own reproductive success. With this assumption, a number of striking parallels between the behavior of humans and other animals are at once explicable.

One suspects that one can assume without presenting all the

evidence that modern man lives in groups larger than that for which the evolutionary process prepared him. Perhaps some of our social turmoil arises from the poor fit. Maybe the unwieldy size of human units today contributes to what we lump together as "future shock."

I believe above all that we should not look back nostalgically for a natural remedy. The past neither can be revived nor relived. In any event, the past is largely a history of the events which got us into the predicament in which we now exist. We should look instead to our own undeveloped capacity for behaving as humans.

In order to retain hope of preserving human freedom and dignity, we must contain and then reduce the human population. We already have done our best to change the natural processes of human population regulation by restraint of wars, curing diseases, combatting poverty, and increasing agricultural productivity.

These are popular activities. We must, however, also address the unpopular, unavoidable consequences. We must change some of human society's most strongly held traditions about marriage and having children.

We also have to change some of the strongly held ideas about rights to use or misuse real estate. The Yankee farmers I grew up with had a folk remedy that worked as long as the community was small. For them a property owner's rights ended when his actions intruded on the freedom of his neighbors.

Although each member of human and other animal populations is in competition with every other member to a greater or lesser degree, unselfish acts do occur. They occur when the individuals involved are sufficiently closely related that by helping the other, one is contributing to the survival of his or her own inherited characteristics (genes). One can calculate (perhaps cynically, but nonetheless accurately) that an animal will act altruistically to the degree that the probable cost of his actions to himself are outweighed by the probable benefit to his own genes (which includes consideration of the proportion of his own genes in the individual benefited).

In closely knit primate troops or human societies, both of which are characteristically made up of extended kin groups, dominant

individuals act responsibly toward other members of the group because of the probability that they will "get it back," either in survival of their own genes or in reciprocal actions by the individuals benefited. The leaders of a troop, tribe or nation may need help some day to fend off the challenges of intruders. To this end, in the small, self-contained communities which have characterized human cultures until recently, there have been abundant opportunities for responsible members of the group to combine to coerce antisocial individuals into acceptable behavior.

During the Forties, Fifties and early Sixties in several small towns in eastern Massachusetts, attitudes sympathetic to coexistence with nature developed by more or less unconscious agreement. The land values stayed low, the roads crooked, incomes various, and lives relatively simple. But these "tweedy" towns have become fashionable. The upwardly mobile have moved in, and the symbols of the status seekers are becoming conspicuous. Impatience with the "inadequate" community services has grown, land prices have skyrocketed, and the concept of stewardship has degenerated to an exclusiveness based on cash flow. This probably will continue. It would be naive for us to expect that a majority of our homogenized and materialistic society would do otherwise.

We need to have communities where people who want the pleasure of association with wildlife can have it and escape the indifference of most suburbanites. In my experience such concern for wildlife is not distributed along lines of wealth, education, or financial condition, and thus it might be politically safe.

We should not neglect the importance of accepted social standards, and the desire of individual people, like other animals, to be included in the social establishment where they live. We might profit by the example of the eminently "establishment" ladies of the eastern seaboard, who in the 1890s decided that they would not wear the feathers of wild birds on their hats. They took a small step which involved minor personal sacrifice, but their example influenced many others, especially those who were socially ambitious. The power of sincere, unyielding social pressure is immense, because ambitious people want to be accepted by the "establishment."

The Other Side of Summer

Around the Fourth of July each year, some obscure change takes place in the northeastern section of the United States and the cities and suburbs begin to drain themselves of their more affluent residents. Some 50,000 of them end up on the island of Martha's Vineyard. By Labor Day they will leave, driven no doubt by the same force that brought them there in the first place. And the winter population, which for two months has mixed with the backbone of the eastern establishment, will return to a more humble existence.

For a number of years, Nancy Safford has been recording this somewhat less flamboyant side of Vineyard life in photographs and interviews. In 1973, she put her efforts together and came out with a book, Time's Island (MIT Press) in which she set down a record of a way of life which began some 350 years ago and is still carrying on today. The photographs in this portfolio are from that book. In some ways they may be a record of a way of life that is passing. But they may also be the future.

*When that spring comes and the sun comes in with them
long days, I can't take being on the mainland.*

Sophia Johnson, 81-year-old resident of Gay Head, quoted in
Time's Island *by Nancy Safford*

Does Wildlife Have a Future?

Our title is of course half a question, because the future of wildlife is inextricably intertwined with that of man. We are both products of an evolving, genetic-ecologic template, but of all the animals, man alone has become clever enough to tinker with the template. We shape the future of the higher organizations of the biosphere as we remake ourselves, and are reshaped in the process. The trouble is that cleverness is a two-edged sword.

This is perhaps too subjective an interpretation, but western man has been incurably subjective. The great danger of subjectivism is that it accepts cultural views as reliable natural history. Without reviewing the history of our ideas about the world and ourselves, it may be pointed out that the new ecological concern of our day, with its emphasis on the symbolic and ecologic role of animals, is a subjective reaction akin to the Romantic movement

By Roland C. Clement
Biologist, vice-president of the National Audubon Society and member of the Massachusetts and National Audubon Joint Scientific Staff.

of the turn of the 19th Century. Here the label "subjective" is not deprecatory, because both these reactions are intuitively sound rejections of the shallow, dangerous self-assurance of science and technology. We must, however, try to see what is happening in more objective terms because the world exists whether we think of it or not; though even our thinking influences it, often more than we know.

We cannot do this without trying to clear away another obstacle. This is the tendency to view everything in nominalistic terms —to let words stand for things instead of remembering that words are symbols for complex processes, and that "things" are arbitrary delimitations of such processes.

This is almost unavoidable, but it is naive. It causes us to believe that a particular, impermanent expression of the life process—a leaf, a tree or a man—is more significant than the process that produces it. We do this because we can see, feel, and taste the leaf, but the process that produced it we can only reconstruct in our minds. We can understand the forest only by studying trees, but this is the problem of which end to look into when using a telescope.

Words forever trap us in the question of the egg and the hen.

For example, we have no great difficulty in agreeing that bald eagles, because they are impressive birds—and partly for this reason our national emblem— ought to be preserved. We have much more trouble agreeing that DDT ought not to be introduced into the environment because its metabolites are cycled in food webs, and, thus, eventually induce undue enzyme formation in female eagles, causing them to lay thin-shelled eggs that break during the incubation process; or even poison the embryo in its egg. And we have trouble because that complex word "environment" includes not only toxins, food webs, and enzymes, but also dollars, votes, and our confused values about the destiny of man.

Ignorance of the past can lead only to naive expectations, because reading the future is the art of projecting the constraints or "givens" of the past as modified by the opportunities of the present. Robert L. Heilbroner, who has been concerned about the survival of our civilization rather than wildlife, wrote a thoughtful book entitled, *The Future As History.* It is a good primer, even for historians of nature.

A long memory, or the ability to reconstruct history, teaches us that the *status quo* is a delusion. If, as some believe, man eliminated the megafauna of North America when he first invaded

this continent, at least 20,000 years ago, it was the first drastic change imposed on wildlife populations by man, even though he had been around a hundred times that long. Others believe that climatic shifts, effecting vegetational change, were the more likely causes of the extinction of the woolly mammoth, sabre-tooth tiger, giant bison, and others.

In any event, we know that timberline, which is now at the latitude of Churchill, Manitoba, has been 400 miles farther south, indicating a colder climate, and 300 miles farther north during the last 10,000 years. Aboriginal man probably had more impact on the landscape than we have been wont to believe, mostly through burning, but he apparently exterminated few species during recent millennia.

Western man, who gained ascendancy in the city states of the Mediterranean basin about 2500 years ago, soon became much more destructive, both directly and indirectly. Especially has this been so in the last century. Whether or not our aggressiveness is due to a misreading of the Biblical injunction to "exercise dominion over the beasts," or to the abandonment of matriarchies, as Robert Graves suggests, it certainly has resulted in a competitive exclusion process that has taken over more and more of the planet for man himself. It is this accelerating trend of destruction we rightly worry about, because it will greatly impoverish world fauna (and flora) if it is not soon reversed.

So long as we were ecologically ignorant, it seemed simple to assume that people are more important than other animals. Certainly, you and I have been brought up to think we are. But today's energy crisis may be a first awakening to the fact that the ecologists are correct when they insist that we are both a product of, and dependent upon, the basic productivity of the ecosystems we occupy. Worse, that we have become parasitic on these systems, because we currently waste fossilized biotic capital, such as petroleum, and degrade ecosystems by polluting them. Excessive human numbers not only impoverish the landscape by oversimplifying the biota (killing off many species), but they impoverish themselves. The proper functioning of ecosystems is assured by the interactions of a multitude of species, a process which then provides surpluses for human consumption and free processing of our wastes. The less leeway there is in natural systems, the more expensive life becomes for people.

The acid rain phenomenon now being experienced on both sides of the North Atlantic, in New England and Scandinavia, is typical of the results of unthinking growth in both human numbers and consumption levels. This unanticipated by-product of pouring sulphur (from coal and oil burning) and nitrates (from automobile combustion) into the atmosphere has, we may expect, already lowered the basic productivity of our northeastern farms, forests, and fisheries by ten percent. Ironically, we are not sure because we have only recently begun measuring such basic productivity. We do know, however, that Russian trawlers are only part of the New England fisherman's problems.

This environmental deterioration begins by "pinching out" those species at the ends of long food chains who, until now, succeeded in life by skimming the surpluses of a healthy pyramid of organisms. Our excesses are eliminating surpluses and truncating the pyramid of numbers, and thus slicing off species like the passenger pigeon, the peregrine falcon, other raptors, trout and salmon, and predatory forms in general. These are usually the long-lived, slowly reproducing species that are not adapted to living in an impoverished or a polluted world. The eutrophication of lakes, and now of bays in the ocean, is exactly such a process of deterioration. Lake Erie and hundreds of other similarly afflicted bodies of water are not "dead;" they have lost their "clean" species and are now dominated by an overabundance of lesser forms, especially algae that "bloom" out of control periodically, because there are too many raw nutrients and not enough grazing species to thin out their ranks before oxygen exhaustion leads to a stinking collapse.

Tragically, instead of nurturing evolutionary experiments and cultural evolution, we make the world more fit for those species whose strategy for survival is based on short generations and large numbers. A multitude of weed species takes over the mutilated niches. Insects and a host of decomposing organisms find our impoverished world much more to their liking than those species we have displaced or are in process of displacing.

In addition, by moving animals about the world—willfully as pets or for other dubious uses, or heedlessly—we are homogenizing biotas, but again favoring weed species—forms that often add as much trouble as interest.

The trends are dire ones, but as already suggested, it would be a mistake to expect them to continue very long. We are, one might say, the first "weed species"

Black-footed ferret

to become aware of its effects on the environment. The mass-consumption demands of our industrial civilization are suicidal and cannot long continue. Tragically, however, people may patch the system long enough to allow it to perpetrate considerably more destruction, against both man and nature. Predictions of collapse for our particular system of "progress," which were viewed as pessimistic just the other day, are indeed the hope of the future, and a basis for optimism if one is interested in a degree of harmony between man and nature. Fortunately, a tripling in the cost of energy may make us design more efficient communities and technologies. Social unrest, resulting from alienation and distributional inequities, may disrupt the whole system of production and cause us to regroup into smaller, almost self-sustained communities. Climatic deterioration, which now seems under way again after half a century of benign climate which facilitated the population explosion, may squeeze out excess human numbers around the planet. Is the tragedy in the retrenchment process or in our failure to preserve leeway?

If this "collapse" of western civilization, partial or complete, directed or undirected, occurs soon, there will be time for a new beginning for us, and a continuation of organic evolution for wildlife. If the reconstruction is delayed, wildlife will be pauperized, and man will be degraded.

We need to learn all over again that civilization is a leavening process that happens to a community of men. It is an approach to an ideal state, never fully achieved. If its commitments are mistaken, as ours have been, it faces a return to barbarism. This is not a new state but a new balance between what is constructive and what is not. R. G. Collingwood, the British philosopher of history, pointed out a generation ago that "To accumulate wealth in order to create by its means a contrast between rich and poor is to use it for the destruction of civilization." This is what we have been about. We have been much too interested in invention, and not enough in conservation: the things to be conserved are our social advances and nature's diversity.

Robin

It turns out, on analysis, that not only is our title half a question, it is almost a non-question. One does not ask dependents about their future.

When we ask about the future of wildlife we usually have in mind certain species of particular interest and concern to us. Since most species have rather specific habitat requirements, we must almost address the prospects of each of these separately if we are to do more than talk in a vacuum. The prospects for the California condor differ greatly from those of the American robin. If we lost ten individual condors next year, we would probably consider the species doomed. We could, however, lose ten million robins without even being aware of it.

The basic lesson is that since wildlife is a product of the land, its future depends on our uses of the land. This is, in turn, dependent upon our own human numbers, our demands (compounded of numbers and lifestyle), the impact of our technology, our social organization, and our attitudes. If we can exercise intelligent control over all these influences, we can help perpetuate most of today's wildlife species for a long time. The most important single contribution to this objective is the reservation of adequate blocks of all the types of habitats produced over the millennia by ecosystem functions, and on which the variety of species depends. These sanctuaries can serve as islands of survival for wildlife while we learn to humanize ourselves.

However, even if we fail to accept responsibility for the perpetuation of all those other life forms which have adventured in time with us these last two million years or so, we will not really end up alone on the planet. Man is tough and adaptable, but many species are tougher and more adaptable than we are. They will survive us. But they won't be those species you and I would enjoy most.

California Condor

91

The State of Maine

Maine is a curious state. Half jammed into Canada, dependent on local resources and tourism for its industries, it is a region which, partly because of its isolation, contains more than its share of natural beauty. That is its strength. But that is also its weakness, because natural beauty is a delicate resource.

The following pages describe the conflict. The photographs are the work of Tom Jones, a free-lance photographer who specializes in the Maine environment. He is now working on a book of photography and each year publishes the Maine Calendar.

Bowdoin Pines

Isle au Haut

Saco

Sugarloaf Area

North Woolwich

Reid State Park

The community of Maine, because such a significant part of it never became industrialized, will survive in better shape than most.

John N. Cole
in the Maine Times

Rights of Ownership or Rights of Use?

The conventional concept of "ownership" in land is detrimental to rational land use, obstructive to the development of related environmental policies, and deceptive to those innocent individuals who would trust it for protection. A new conceptual basis for land use law and policy is required to reconcile the legitimate rights of the users of land with the interest of society in maintaining a high quality environment. This essay is intended to promote discussion of ways to reconcile these objectives.[1]

Were the prevailing legal concepts of land ownership in the United States not already established, it is highly improbable that any similar body of doctrine would develop; rather, law more appropriate to modern social and economic realities would evolve. The existing aggregation of laws and practices pertaining to land ownership and use are beneficial primarily to persons interested in exploitation or litigation. They provide little protection to the owner who lacks continuous economic and legal counsel and who is unable personally to influence political decisions. Moreover, the laws are even less helpful to communities and the general public in maintaining or restoring the quality of the environment.

The persistence of archaic concepts of ownership rights is possibly the principal obstacle to effective land use planning. A redefinition of the rights flowing to an individual from his ownership in land is thus a necessary concomitant to land use planning, as well as to environmental management. Land law rooted in the conventions of Tudor England cannot be expected to serve the needs of the post-industrial society now emerging.

The Confusing Legacy of Conventional Land "Ownership"

In his essay on "Control of the Use of Land in English Law," W. O. Hart, then Clerk of the London County Council, observed:

"The English Law of real property never developed a true theory of ownership: title was, and still is in essence, possessory and, moreover, relative rather than absolute."[2] The prevailing principles, terminologies, and deficiencies of English land law were transplanted to colonial America, and, although changed circumstances led to changed concepts and practices, the basic elements of law as interpreted in seventeenth and eighteenth century England have continued to influence land law and policy in the United States. The absence of an adequate theory of land ownership and the status of man-land relationships at the time of the English colonization of America were basic forces which have shaped the tough resistance of the American political-legal system to effective public control over the uses of land.

Throughout the history of law in Western society, property in land has been distinguished from other forms of property, and rights of ownership have been distinguished from rights of use. Rights pertaining to land have never been absolute in fact, and only rarely in theory. As R. G. Crocombe observes, "The word ownership is misleading. A person does not really own land: he owns rights in land."[3] Authority over the uses and disposition of land has always been residual in society, whether represented by the community,

By Lynton K. Caldwell
Arthur F. Bentley Professor of Political Science and Professor of Public and Environmental Affairs, Indiana University, Bloomington, Indiana

101

the monarch, or the state, and survives today in the concept of "eminent domain."

Except as allocated to specific persons for designated uses, land in Anglo-Saxon England was "folcland," that is, belonging to the folk.[4] Under feudalism, distinctions between the rights of ownership and of use continued. As the English economy outgrew the provisions of the common law for the adjudication of disputes over the uses of land, however, the Court of Chancery, where adjudication was not rigidly bound by precedent and tradition, assumed increasing importance. Although Parliament in 1535 enacted the Statute of Uses to clarify and reconcile the complexities which had accumulated regarding rights in the conveyance, utilization, and alienation of land, economic forces and legal conservatism soon combined to diminish public benefit from this legislation. As a result, the legacy of English land law that was transmitted to the American colonies was highly technical, complex, and unsystematic. Moreover, since real property law is a province of the individual states, its unsystematic complexity has increased over the years—its deficiencies remaining largely unresolved.

The period of the European colonization of America witnessed a transition in the status of man-land relationships from vestiges of feudal land tenure to the treatment of land as a marketable commodity. The transition continued over several centuries and was influenced by economic forces and opportunities, rather than by a theory or master plan. In America the great opportunity lay on the frontier, where land was free from the traditional encumbrances of communal, seignorial, or royal authority. The possession of land conferred security, economic freedom, and social status, and the settler in America developed a deep hunger for ownership of land such as he could never have hoped to satisfy in the Old World. As an owner of land, he owed no obligation to neighbor or posterity, and very little to the state. He came closer to holding his land in "fee simple absolute" in a literal sense than anyone ever has under Anglo-American law.

Freed of the vestigial constraints of feudalism, the landholder in America developed a tenacious attitude toward unfettered rights of private land ownership. Most important of these was the right to treat land as a commodity—to buy and sell, to speculate, and, under the right of ownership, to take from the land whatever might be of value. This strong sense of a private right of ownership combined with the abundance of unpreempted land and the disinclination of government to interfere with land use to establish a tradition of private property in land that has proved highly resistant to the imposition of public land use controls. With a few exceptions pertaining chiefly to public nuisances, the rights of ownership fully covered the rights to use or to dispose. No other society appears to have gone so far in leaving the fate of the land to the discretion of the private owner.

The development of public land use policy in the United States thus began inauspiciously with a people emotionally committed to a myth of private rights in land ownership. Although the pressures on available land caused by an increasing population and expanding economy have somewhat eroded the commitment to this extreme form of economic individualism, public opinion has continued to adhere to its basic tenets. Whether the refusal to examine underlying concepts stems from a conscious fear of the effect of possible alternatives or merely from a subconscious sense of tradition, the effect has been the frustration of the rational use of land in the long-range public interest and oftentimes the failure to protect the interests of the individual landowner.

Anomalies and Deficiencies of the Ownership Concept

The case for conventional ownership of land cannot be made by reference to history or theory. The history of American land law and its English antecedents makes evident that the right to hold, enjoy, develop, and protect land, as well as to profit from its use, was never absolute nor contingent upon ultimate legal ownership. The strongest defense for the prevailing concept of land ownership is the empirical fact of its existence. American folklore vaguely envisioned a moral right in lawful possession that stood against all claims except those of the state for taxes and those of creditors to whom the land had been mortgaged. The doctrine of eminent domain (the government's power to claim private land for use by or for the public), however, involved a concomitant recognition that the ultimate owner of land was the society as a whole. Moreover, the myth of a moral right to absolute possession is not generally supported by interpretations of natural law, nor uniformly by the idea of absolute possession as a civil right. There are advantages in the private ownership concept which account for its persistence, but not all of these advantages are derived from the mere fact of ownership; there are a number of contingencies for which ownership offers at best a partial solution.

Legal fact and popular concept are seldom entirely consistent in any field of law. With respect to land, the fixation on private property has tended to obscure the reality that peaceful possession rests upon the public affirmation and protection of whatever rights do in fact exist. If privacy is an objective, land ownership does not assure it. The privacy of an owner may be invaded by public authorities for many reasons, among them tax assessments and a myriad of public uses such as highways and airports. Nor is ownership a barrier against such effects of modern civilization as noise, glare, litter, and atmospheric pollution.

The rights of ownership being conditional, the practical question of the meaning of ownership consequently relates to the conditions under which alleged rights of owners may be, or would be, enforceable. At best, ownership supports a right to sue for damages or injunctive relief. In most communities, defense against casual trespass is a responsibility of the owner, not of the local government through the police, and the owner's ability to enforce his rights is limited by law, and often by circumstance.

It is logically anomalous to concepts of private ownership in land, but nevertheless a fact, that many state laws confer upon privately owned utilities the power of eminent domain over privately owned real property. If the exercise of this public power is essential to the siting of power plants and the routing of transmission lines, it is dubious that the generation and distribution of electrical energy is an appropriate activity for private enterprise. It would be more consistent with popular concepts of private property rights if eminent domain were invoked only by agents of the public. Logically, the sites and routes of power lines, pipelines, and generating plants would be publicly owned; if operation was through private enterprise, the use of leases or franchises to the utility from the government would be appropriate.

Just as conventional concepts of land ownership cannot assure privacy, they cannot guarantee personal and economic security. It is not uncommon for an individual to be murdered or robbed on his own land, the market value of land may fall as well as rise, and the burdens of ownership may be increased through taxation and special assessments. The relative permanence of land does make it acceptable collateral for loans, and this economic advantage, together with the relative stability of land values, offers the most reliable benefit to be obtained from ownership as presently defined. Any such benefit, however, is obtainable only to the extent that land is treated as a commodity and is enjoyed exclusively by the owner, often at the expense of his neighbors and society generally.

Although some laws governing nuisances and threats to public safety have traditionally limited the lawful uses to which an owner may put his land, these limitations pertain to the use, and not the ownership, of land. It is at this point, where rights of use are claimed to follow from the rights of ownership, that legal and political conflict over the rights of use characteristically arise. Although the principal advantage of land ownership has been in concomitant freedoms of use, especially to sell or otherwise convey for a consideration, the most numerous and flagrant abuses of land tend to be associated with its treatment as a commodity. Some of the worst practices are perpetrated by corporations engaged in land sales and speculation. Ironically, the same transaction by such an enterprise which proves economically profitable to a stockholder may, unknown to him at the time, result in a serious loss of what he considers valuable environmental amenities.

The composite picture of land ownership rights in the United States is anything but consistent. The basic deficiency in the law of land ownership lies in the inadequacy of its philosophic foundation. It is difficult to build a logical case for, or against, a body of law which has grown, virtually ad hoc, in response to pressures and events. As K. E. Digby observed with respect to the evolution of the English law of real property: "[T]he nature and attributes of the various classes of rights are to be accounted for by reference rather to their history than to any principles of jurisprudence." [5] Digby concluded that the confusion engendered by provisions of the Statute of Uses "renders any real simplification of the law of real property impossible, without a more thorough rebuilding of the whole structure from its foundations and the substitution of a systematic or scientific for a historical classification. . . ." [6] Since Digby's time, significant rationalization, if not any real simplification, has occurred in English law, notably through the Town and Country Planning Acts. In the United States, however, there are as many different systems of land law as there are states and their 10,000 local subdivisions, with additional legislation pertaining to federal lands and territories. Of course, the mere fact of variation does not in itself imply deficiency; it does, however, reflect the absence in American society of a guiding philosophy of man-land relationships.

The closest Anglo-American law could come to developing an adequate theoretical foundation for rights of land ownership and use was a very inadequate approximation to such a theory provided by the doctrine of natural law. The most influential American expositor of natural law doctrine in relation to land was Thomas Jefferson.[7] His opinions, however, tended to be broadly philosophical and political, rather than more narrowly jurisprudential, and frequently embraced contradictory propositions for which he offered no resolution. Jefferson argued that the system of land inherited from Norman England could not be applied to colonial America without the consent of its inhabitants. He compared the European settlers of America to the Saxon invaders of Britain, declaring: "Their own blood was spilt in acquiring lands for their settlements, their own fortunes expended in making settlement effectual; for themselves they fought, for themselves they conquered, and for themselves alone they have a right to hold." [8]

Jefferson thus alleged that the British crown had no claim to title of unoccupied lands in the colonies and that their use and disposition by the Americans were justified by conquest and occupancy. This taking of possession of unoccupied land appeared to be a natural right, but, reasoning that even natural rights could be abridged or modified with the consent of the people or their deputies, Jefferson believed that the personal ownership of property must be deemed a civil rather than natural right. Although he believed that society should guarantee to everyone "a free exercise of his industry, and the fruits acquired by it," [9] he held that the rights of an individual, natural or civil, never extended to harming the equal rights of others.

Moreover, Jefferson did not believe that the civil law of one generation could bind succeeding generations. "Each generation," he wrote, "has the usufruct of the earth during the period of its continuance. When it ceases to exist, the usufruct passes on to the succeeding generation, free and unencumbered, and so on successively, from one generation to another forever." [10] Beyond the obvious consideration that every generation to some extent reinterprets existing policies and laws, this philosophic proposition was hardly applicable in the practical world and was clearly not supportive of conventional practices regarding land ownership.

Thus, the man who, more than any other, may be described as the father of American democratic ideals left a confusing legacy of thought regarding the rights of the individual and the rights of society vis-à-vis the ownership and use of land. No other public figure in the formative years of the nation had greater concern for land policy and for the rights of the individual farmer and homesteader. The persistence of his ideas in a populous, industrial, and interdependent society has had effects he could hardly have imagined and many of which have been utterly inconsistent with his values. Nevertheless, his insistence upon the need for the adaptability of law and institutions to the changing circumstances of society is the clearest and most pertinent contribution of his thought to the present debate over land use policy and law.

Needed: A New Conceptual Basis

The conventional belief that land may be "owned" as of "right" rather than as a socially derived privilege is undercut by a number of considerations, several of which have shaped land-use arrangements in other societies. Common among primitive and pastoral peoples, for example, is the belief that because no man made the land, no man may possess it as his "own." This viewpoint, which has been adopted in some sectors of the ecology/environmental quality movement, is totally unrelated to Marxist theory, being derived from a theory of man-environment relations rather than from socio-economic philosophy. Although in exceptional instances land may be "made" in the sense of being made available for human use through human effort, any one individual rarely is equal to the task. Thus, the polders of the Netherlands, which were socially engineered, "belong" to the nation.

A second consideration which has persisted throughout the evolution of the law of real property involves the contrast of the transiency of man in time and space against the relative permanence of land. This consideration, indeed, is the basis for distinctions between real and personal property. Since real property cannot be separated from its environment and since successive generations will depend upon it for sustenance, the integrity of the land and its ecosystems demands that the arbitrary personal use of any part of it be subject to social interposition if the acts of an owner pose a threat to the continuing welfare of the community.

From this consideration follows the principle of stewardship, under which ownership or possession of land is viewed as a trust, with attendant obligations to future generations as well as to the present. [11] The ownership concept as it developed in the United States emphasized the rights of personal possession but suggested no attitude of responsibility to the public or to posterity. Beyond the law, however, there has been recognition of an ethical concept of stewardship. Although the roots of this attitude, which at times assume a semireligious or mystical character, [12] are ancient and multicultural, its assumptions regarding man as belonging to the totality of nature are more consistent with reality as revealed by science than are the technical principles of judicial logic evolved in response to the exigencies of economics and political power.

A fourth consideration with respect to land ownership, having no historical tradition, is that the ownership concept developed under relatively constant social conditions entailing no massive rapid changes in land value or usage. In America the relative abundance of cheap land and the minimal demands of society upon landowners continued from the time of the European settlements until the late nineteenth century. By the mid-twentieth century, however, radical changes in man-land relationships were effected by great increases in population and per capita wealth. The impact of technology upon land use was no less dramatic, new modes of transportation making every part of the nation readily accessible to popular use and exploitation. Air-conditioning and cheap energy altered human ecology and land use patterns over large areas of the nation. Following World War II, the escalating market value of land had an impact on American society equalled only by the concomitant destruction of the landscape and the generally disastrous dispersion of housing and commercial activities over the countryside. The cumulative effect of these changes has been to bring into question the social desirability of the rights of land ownership as presently construed. The case for ownership of land would be stronger were the personal freedom and independence of most Americans actually dependent upon it. The present status of land ownership, however, is beneficial chiefly to developers and speculators, as well as to exploiters of values attached to the land. While to the individual home owner mere ownership offers little more than the illusion of security, the advantages accrue to the indifferent despoiler of the land and landscape whose interest is with neither land nor environment but rather with the economic returns from his land transactions.

Together, these considerations suggest that a more appropriate mechanism than conventional ownership is required to govern and ensure the right to use land in particular ways and for particular purposes and the ability to obtain reliable protection, consistent with the public interest, from invasion of such right. Systematic means are needed to balance the various uses of land in society. The proposition guiding any such alternative should be that, next to man, land is the fundamental element of the human environment and the one most important in shaping the character of society.

The need for a change in laws governing land arises as a concomitant of other major social changes. English land law experienced periods of major change at critical junctures in English history. The change from a communal to a feudal land system followed the Norman Conquest and from feudal to commercial, illustrated by the Statute of Uses, marked the birth of modern England. The third dramatic change occurred when England reached "saturation" with respect to demands upon land and when social and ecological considerations gained ascendancy over market considerations. The series of Property Acts taking effect in 1926 and the subsequent Town and County Planning Acts have restated and restricted the rights of the landowner, although, in a characteristically English manner, the changes have been incremental and reformist rather than expressive of a radical new ideology.

English land law was transplanted to America at a time when the powers inherent in private land ownership had reached a zenith. The conditions favoring free exercise of such powers have continued for over 300 years, becoming deeply ingrained in American ethics, attitudes, and expectations. Radical changes in the American economy and lifestyles in the mid-twentieth century found the nation poorly equipped by psychology or by law to cope with the rapidly mounting problems of land use. The persistence of the traditional land ownership concept in the face of such vastly altered societal circumstances represents perhaps the most costly deficiency of the traditional concept—its inability to adapt to meet changing circumstances. Cheap energy, together with a free market in land, have encouraged the disintegration of cities and the sprawl of economic activities and settlements across the country, entailing heavy fixed costs in public services and transportation of people and materials and involving attendant losses of environmental amenities. The energy crisis of recent months demonstrates the manner in which the decentralizing effect of land use policies has defeated the efficient use of mass transit in suburban areas.

The cumulative effect of the most recent quarter-century of private land use decisions has been the disintegration of the physical structure of American society. These decisions have, of course, been influenced, often inadvertently, by public policies relating to taxes, credit, highway construction, low-cost housing, and civil rights. An interlocking set of conditions and policies devised to deal with them have converged to destroy urban as well as rural environments and to overwhelm the burgeoning suburbs with expenses and problems. It is in the face of this disintegration of the social fabric that land use planning and the control of urban growth have at last become major subjects of political concern. In the absence of a fundamental change in the rights of land ownership, however, serious efforts to implement rational land use planning legislation are likely to be ineffectual.

Some Elements of a Rational Policy

In the search for alternative principles of land policy, it is essential that temporary economic advantages (or disadvantages) to particular individuals be distinguished from definable long-range benefits satisfying social and ecological criteria. It also is necessary to distinguish theory from actual effect. Failure to make these distinctions would almost certainly increase the probability of opposition from persons owning land even though many of the traditional rights of ownership would be replaced by rights of use. If those rights of ownership presumed to ensure the security and responsibility of the individual landowner could be maintained more effectively in some other way, there might be a generally recognized advantage in abandoning the concept of land ownership. Thus, assured protection of the socially and ecologically harmless rights which now are allegedly protected by ownership would certainly be a prerequisite to the willing acceptance by landowners of any new set of legal principles under which land itself is not owned.

A second prerequisite would be provision against the "tragedy of the commons" effect.[13] Land, as such, would be no more "ownable" than air or water, but the *uses* of land would be the object of law and of rights, as presently is the case with water. The objective would not be to substitute bureaucratic for commercial decision-making over land use but rather to clarify and specify this decisional process, as well as to assure more adequate protection to the legitimate interests of individuals and the present and long-term needs of society.

Following are some propositions, none of which is intrinsically new, which might serve toward these purposes. Any element of novelty lies in the combination of these propositions to form a new conceptual basis for land law and policy, the goal being the construction of a foundation in jurisprudence for the environmental policies which must be devised to safeguard our future in a finite world.

First, rights of ownership should be redefined to apply not to land itself but to specific rights to occupy or use particular parcels of land, or both, in accordance with publicly established criteria. Rights to use might be bought and sold, and could confer possession, but the land itself would cease to be the representative symbol of these rights. The ultimate repository for such rights would be in society, and their administration, while through government, could involve extensive citizen participation.

Second, rights of occupancy would be defined by law, with land classified according to its economic and ecological capabilities, and would be regulated by provisions specifying the obligations of occupancy and governing the acquisition of additional rights. The term "rights" would encompass those activities in relation to the land in which the occupant or user might freely engage, as well as those aspects of privacy and of security from external damage or annoyance which society through government would undertake to defend and protect. Obligations concomitant to custody of land would include, in addition to traditional restrictions against public nuisance, measures designed to protect air and water quality, the integrity of ecosystems, and the character of the landscape, whether man-made or natural. The classification system, allocating specific rights to particular areas or parcels of land, would be the product of public planning. For any given piece of land, only those rights allocated to it could be exercised, although not all available rights would have to be exercised. Furthermore, a purchaser might buy some but not all of the rights pertaining to a parcel of land; he could, for example, purchase the right to farm without also obtaining the rights to mine or to develop the land. The combination of rights and obligations thus defined could apply to communities and public authorities, as well as individuals and corporations. Such application would be especially important with respect

to land used for public works, such as power plants, energy transmission lines, airports, highways, military installations, scientific research, recreation, historic preservation, and natural resources development.

Finally, taxation would apply to the economic value of the rights actually possessed and exercised, not to the land itself or in anticipation of rights that *might* be obtained for the particular piece of land. The tax rate could be adjusted to compensate the public for any burden, such as air pollution, that a particular land use might place upon a community. This system would put an end to the practice of assessing land at its presumed market value regardless of its use. The owner of the right to farm a tract of land, for example, could be taxed only in relation to that right, even though the farm was surrounded by land for which highly taxed development rights had been granted. In addition, since capital gains in land per se would not be obtainable, the owner of the right to farm a piece of land could not follow the present practice of holding land off the market in anticipation of an increase in its value. He could not develop the land or sell development rights to others unless he possessed such rights, and any changes in the use of land not included among the

rights already possessed by the user would require purchase of additional rights from the appropriate public authority. Conversion of farmland to an industrial site, for instance, would require the purchase of a right or franchise to develop. The assessment of rights would reflect the profitability of the development and the costs and benefits to the community. In this regard, the right to remove minerals, soil, or timber from land would require conditional permits drafted to protect ecological and amenity values and to ensure the economical handling of the materials. This arrangement would replace existing severance taxation.

A major objective of these changes in land law would be to assure that publicly created values in land would accrue to the public. Thus, increases in the value of land at newly constructed interchanges on interstate highways would afford no opportunity for profit to the existing land users. Whether development rights or franchises would be granted would depend upon considerations of areal physical planning and public necessity and convenience. A development franchise could not be granted without an environmental impact study and, if granted, could stipulate style of construction, siting, landscaping, and provision for traffic flow and public utilities.

Surrender of development rights, and avoidance of attendant financial liabilities, would require restoration of land to a condition at least equivalent, in most cases, to its predevelopment status. Derelict billboards, abandoned buildings, mines, quarries, and other residuals of discontinued development would be taxed at rates sufficient to compel their owners to undertake remedial or restorative measures. The intent of these provisions would be to make development more responsible and more carefully considered. It would also make development less spontaneous and less profitable to would-be speculators. Special provision should be made, however, to prevent the destruction of potentially useful structures or of buildings of artistic or historic value. Certificates of exemption might be issued to relieve owners of these nonproductive "improvements" from taxation at development rates.

A secondary purpose of the proposed changes would be prevention of socially and ecologically harmful speculation in development. Although a grant of development rights would confer limited authority to change the uses of land in certain ways, major environmental changes, such as development of a shopping center involving public services and transportation, would require an additional franchise. If, as has been suggested, development taxes must be paid as long as a right to development is held, developers could not escape errors of judgment or miscarriage of projects merely by abandoning them. Until the development rights were sold or surrendered, they would continue as liabilities accruing against the holder. Some form of public receivership would doubtless be necessary to take custody of abandoned property and to restore the land with funds obtained from forfeited equities or from penalties for the failure to restore the land.

A virtue of the foregoing approach to land use policy is that decisions affecting the public would in effect become public decisions, a circumstance that occurs imperfectly, if at all, under the laws currently prevailing in most states. The decisional process could be made more open and explicit than generally is the case under the system of private land ownership. The "rights to use" approach would direct public action away from litigation and toward planning and administration.

Among the probable effects of removing land per se from the market and from treatment as a commodity would be a temporary price instability until completion of redefinition of rights in terms of use. Although in the interim prices of land would probably be depressed, a traumatic effect on the real estate economy might be avoided if the existing market value were redefined to be the value of its present use. The immediate effect of the proposed changes on expansive economic growth would be negative; the long-range impact, however, would be to stabilize economic activity and reduce the incidence of failure in land development projects. In terms of the effect upon the public revenues, taxation of land would be replaced by taxation of rights in land. Structures built on the land could, as at present, be taxed separately. The incidence of these taxes would require careful study, since there would be no inevitable direction in which the tax burden could be shifted.

Feasibility of These Propositions

The principal effect of the foregoing propositions would be to take from private persons, individual or corporate, the power to effect significant alterations in the environment without public consent. It does not follow, however, that the power of environmental planning and management would be transferred to public bureaucracy. Use of citizen boards of review and open planning sessions, as well as provision for input from science and the design arts, could result in more socially and ecologically responsible land use decisions than might be expected under the existing technicalities of land use law.

The objectives of these propositions are, in a very fundamental sense, conservative. They are intended to preserve and to conserve, to encourage and to enforce responsibility toward society and posterity, and to reduce the likelihood of rash and destructive uses of land and resources. Moreover, they are intended to do these things without loss to the real freedoms currently enjoyed under ownership of land, except where their exercise would be prejudicial to society.

It should be apparent that the proposal to replace rights of land ownership with rights of use implies the possibility of major changes in the power structure of society and in the processes of decision-making with respect to land use. These changes are certainly not imminent; to what extent might they become feasible?

The propositions which have been suggested may, in certain respects, appear similar to those advanced more than a century ago by Henry George.[14] The philosophical foundation of both approaches is ecological and stems from the belief that, in a logical and meaningful sense, land, as such, can no more be owned than air or water. The purpose of the propositions advanced in this Article, however, is more limited than that of George's, and the alternatives are more numerous, more complex, and less definite.

No general reformist device such as the "single tax" is proposed, nor would the tax on uses suggested in this Article necessarily force land into economic productivity or cause it to be withheld from use. It is the value of the use that would be taxed, not the value of the land. Payments for rights of use correspond to Henry George's "rent," and, although no claim is made that this form of taxation is necessarily more equitable than those presently practiced in the United States, it may be suggested that the effects of taxation might be clarified and criteria for equitability more adequately defined.

Whatever its deficiencies, the existing system of land ownership, and its variations and modifications, has produced relationships and results that are generally, if imperfectly, understood. Remedies exist for most abuses, although their practical availability is often expensive and belated. Substitution of another system of law for man-land relationships will not be easily accomplished. This Article has advanced the proposition that the changes which have been occurring in modern society have made the present land ownership system increasingly disfunctional to rational economic and ecological objectives. Nevertheless, recourse to a different system should be undertaken only after careful study of the probable consequences of such a change.

The importance of research on the relationships between land use and the laws governing proprietary land units has been stressed by D. R. Denman, Professor of Land Economy at the University of Cambridge.[15] Study of the proprietary structures in land and of relationships between the proprietary land unit (ownership) and the enterprise unit (use) has been undertaken by the National Institute of Agrarianical Research, Rural Economy and Research in France.[16] The problem of finding an optimal relationship between rights of ownership and rights of use thus is not unique to the United States.

Professor Denman in his inaugural lecture declared: "Property rights in land or rights analogous to them are, in the last analysis, the only power by which men can execute positive plans for the use of land and natural resources."[17] Denman argues persuasively that much of the frustration and failure in present land use planning has resulted from the failure of planners to recognize adequately "the positive influence of property rights in land" and that "the planning process has not superseded the property sanction."[18] The apparent need is to find an appropriate institutional means for reconciling the right of the individual to own with the need of society to plan. Rights of ownership in land as they have been conventionally interpreted in the United States have not met this need. The wise course would therefore seem to be to identify those analogous rights which, even if retaining the terminology

of private property rights in land, would redefine those rights to serve better the public interest.

Reprinted by permission of the author and the William and Mary Law Review, *appearing in Volume 15, Number 4, Summer 1974. Copyright 1974 by the Marshall-Wythe School of Law, College of William and Mary, Williamsburg, Virginia 23185.*

1 For a general treatment of land in American society, see M. Clawson, America's Land and Its Uses (1972).

2 Law and Land 23 (C. Haar ed. 1964).

3 South Pacific Commission, Improving Land Tenure: A Survey of the Problems of Adapting Customary Land Tenure Systems to Modern Economic Conditions in the Region Served by the South Pacific Commission (1968).

4 For the history of English land law, see K. Digby, An Introduction to the History of the Law of Real Property (1875); W. Holdsworth, An Historical Introduction to the Land Law (1927); A. Simpson, An Introduction to the History of the Land Law (1961).

5 K. Digby, *supra* note 4, at vi.

6 *Id.*

7 *See* Caldwell, *The Jurisprudence of Thomas Jefferson,* 18 Ind. L.J. 193 (1943).

8 2 The Works of Thomas Jefferson 64-65 (P. Ford ed. 1904).

9 *Id.*

10 *Id.* at 298 (letter to John Wayles Eppes, June 24, 1813).

11 *See* C. Little & R. Burnap, Stewardship: The Land, the Landowner, the Metropolis (1965) (prepared for landowners in the New York Metropolitan region by the Open Space Action Committee).

12 *See* L. Bailey, The Holy Earth (1919).

13 *See* Hardin, *The Tragedy of the Commons,* Science, Dec. 13, 1968, at 1243.

14 *See* H. George, Our Land and Land Policy (1871); H. George, Progress and Poverty (1879).

15 D. Denman, Land Use and the Constitution of Property: An Inaugural Lecture (1969).

16 *See* Brun, *Droits de Propriete et Droits d'Usage du Sal Agricole: Un Essai de Description, Economie Rurale* (No. 75, 1968).

17 D. Denman, *supra* note 15, at 2.

18 *Id.*

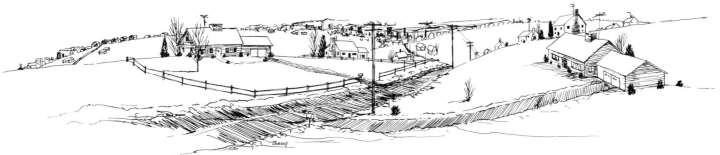

An Alternative Future

It has been suggested that the legal and cultural changes
in attitudes towards the land which are now taking place,
and those which will occur between now and the 21st Century
have never been equalled in the history of western civilization.
What this will mean in terms of actual land use practices
remains to be seen. And what this means as far as the use of
future technologies remains to be seen. But one thing is
certain. If only half the changes that took place between
the turn of the century and the present occur between now
and the 21st Century, the world we know will indeed be turned
upside down. What this new world will look like is up to us.
Fortunately, we still have a choice.

Wyoming coal strip mine

James J. MacKenzie

Suburban development   Framingham, Massachusetts   Richard Kahn

Suburban non-development   *Conservation land in Lincoln, Massachusetts*   *Hal Morgan*

Rural landscape

Daniel S. Brody

Urban landscape   *Eric Myrvaagnes*

Suburban parking

Mary S. Shakespeare

British Rail's Advanced Passenger Train (APT)

Henry Glover's wind-powered tool mill   W. Dedham, Massachusetts   1890